STAYING REAL

The Millennials Guide to Home Buying

VANESSA PATTERSON

Table of Contents

Introduction

So you want to buy a home, but you're not necessarily willing to give up your first born, your left leg, and every dollar you own. Understandable.

Buying a home can be stressful enough as it is, but many millennial are facing a unique set of obstacles. Ask a millennial what they consider to be some of their biggest barriers to the home-buying process and you're likely to hear one or more of these answers:

- "Student loan payments. Sallie Mae won't let me break up with her": For millennials who are fresh out of college and are not yet established in their careers, student loan bills can be a problem. Simple expenses like rent, utilities, and car payments can easily become a burden when you're expected to practically hand over your check to Big Brother Loan Collector.

- "I like to go out and have fun. If that means spending a little money, then so be it": There aren't too many millennials who will tell you that they *don't* like to go out and have fun. The key to navigating the murky waters of having a good time and being reckless with money is to create a reasonable budget.

Many a millennial has fallen victim to letting one too many drinks dictate whether or not the light bill gets paid.

- "I'm happy where I'm at. I've been renting my apartment for years, and am not ready to give it up": Some millennials are in a sound financial position, but merely do not realize the advantages to buying a home. They've been comfortable for so long that they don't understand just how much money they are losing from being a years-on-end renter.

- "Buying a home is a big commitment...I can't even remember to take the trash out on trash days. I don't think I'm ready": Buying a home *is* a big commitment, and some millennials are more than mature enough to realize this.

- "I don't know how even to begin buying a home": Some millennials don't want to jump into the home-buying process blind. This also is understandable. Lucky for you, I've got just the guide.

The home-buying process boils down to this simple principle: If you're prepared and know what to expect, the entire process becomes less stressful and more predictable.

When you're driving, to know where you're going, it's important to know how to get there. It's crucial to have a map or some navigation to guide you in the right direction.

Consider this home-buying guide for millennials your personal GPS.

Chapter 1: Buying vs. Renting: Why Buying a Home Makes Sense

It's the advice that's been engrained into your psyche like an ominous tape recorder on repeat: You need to stop throwing your money away with renting. You need to buy a home. Buy a home. Buy a home.

It's also a nugget of wisdom that the Baby Boomer generation is famous for pushing. But, is it true? Is buying a home a better option than renting for years on end?

The short answer is yes. Here are a few reasons why:

When you buy a home, you are investing money

When you rent an apartment, you are giving away money. Once you buy a home, you start to accumulate what's called equity. Equity is money that's left over after you pay the balance of what you owe on the house. For example, if you owe your lender $100,000.00 on your home, and your home is worth $120,000.00, you'd have a free and clear $20,000.00 in equity. You could either sell your home to get this money or borrow against it with a loan. When you are a renter, you are not accumulating or saving money. Equity simply does not exist for renters.

Inflation hits renters much harder than it does homeowners

When the cost of goods rises, often, so do rent prices. Homeowners with a fixed mortgage rate never face this problem. Your mortgage payment each month will never change, even if the market does. You can take pride in knowing that even as your friends' rent prices are increasing; your mortgage payments are staying the same (and often, decreasing depending on whether or not you choose to refinance.

The homeowner and renter mind-sets are real things

Homeowners have a vested interest in maintaining their property and their neighborhoods. They realize that the better the property and neighborhood is, the more their house is worth. Homeowners do *not* want to lose the equity in their homes, so they work to preserve it.

While renters may have the same desire to live in better neighborhoods, unlike homeowners, their desire isn't motivated by saving money (and we all know how big of a motivator money can be, right?). A renter who walks past an empty soda can sit on the sidewalk essentially has nothing to lose; that's not so much the case with a homeowner. The homeowner has quite a bit to lose.

If people perceive the neighborhood as one that's littered with trash, that homeowner's property value—and that homeowner's *neighbor's* property value—decreases. For this reason, homeowners tend to be much more careful about the upkeep of their homes and neighborhoods, which means a better living situation for you.

A landlord can (and often does) put any ol' appliance in your apartment

As a homeowner, you have complete control of what type of home improvements you make. Let's say your refrigerator goes out. If you're a renter, you'd tell your landlord, and your landlord would either choose to repair your current refrigerator or opt to get a different one. Notice how I did not say that your landlord would opt to get a *new* one. That's because, often, things don't quite work out that way.

Many landlords substitute appliances that aren't working with refurbished items to cut down on costs. And, you aren't exactly guaranteed to like the look or feel of the refurbished item. So, that pink and red zebra striped refurbished fridge that your landlord just got you? You're keeping it. End of story. But, if you're a homeowner, you are free to replace anything in your house as you please. In many cases, remodeling or replacing appliances increases the value of your home, which in turn increases your equity.

Approaching the home-buying process with an optimistic attitude is a must if you're going to have a pleasant and smooth experience. Be cognizant of your budget and how things might change for you as a homeowner. You might just find that being a homeowner is more advantageous for your financial situation than you think.

Chapter 2: Reducing your Tax Liability

Now that you're aware of a few of the surface-level advantages of buying a house, you should know about one more major one: Buying a home reduces your tax liability. To translate, when you buy a home, you save money at tax time. Homeowners pay interest on their mortgage loans. This interest is tax deductible. Homeowners also pay property taxes which is tax deductible.

Buying Home

Buying a home is an appealing option for those who want a tax shelter. When you're renting, Uncle Sam looks at your income and takes it for what it is. If you made $65,000.00 for the year, you'd pay taxes on $65,000.00. But, if you're a homeowner *and* you're paying taxes and interest on your home loan, you have the privilege of writing off the interest that you've paid for that tax year which could save you thousands at tax time.

If you're a business owner who works from home, you're really in luck. A home office, along with all of your home office expenses (e.g. internet, telephone, etc.) is all deductible at tax time.

These are all benefits that you simply do not get when you're a renter. If you can afford it, and you've worked out a budget that fits your lifestyle, homeownership is much easier on the pockets at tax time.

Chapter 3: Finding the Perfect Realtor

Gone are the days when Realtors were only little old ladies with cheetah-print scarves and bad short-term memories. Good realtors come in all ages and experience levels. A Realtor can make or break your home-buying experience, so it's important to choose one who you can trust. Here are three key things to be leery of when it comes time to choose your realtor

Lack of Flexibility

When it comes to selecting a dealer, experience doesn't always dictate quality. Some realtors with years and years of experience can be set in their ways and rigid when it comes to navigating the home-buying process. There is no one-shoe-fits-all solution when it comes to buying a home. Every person's financial situation is unique. It's best to find a realtor who is willing to work with you to find the best home and payment options for your situation.

An Unfamiliarity with the Neighborhood

Would you go to an electronics store and start asking the store clerk about 2% milk? Would you go to the grocery store to ask the cashier about an iPad that you're thinking about purchasing? Hopefully not! Store clerks aren't just any old clerks. They all have specialized stores that they work in. These stores make them experts in specific areas.

An electronics store clerk might not know much about 2% milk, but a grocery store clerk would. A grocery store clerk may not be familiar with iPad specs, but a clerk from an electronics store would be. The same principle applies to realtors. Realtors have certain neighborhoods that they are familiar with and certain other neighborhoods that they only vaguely know about. When you're choosing a realtor, it's important to pick one who is familiar with the neighborhood you're looking to move to.

You want someone who can give you the ins and outs of what goes on in your area, not someone simply looking to sell a house. A lot of people make the mistake of going with a realtor who is a friend or a relative.

This is fine if the realtor knows your target area very well. Although, often, this isn't the case. Stick to the realtors who have experience with buying or selling homes in your chosen neighborhood.

Impulsiveness

This time, I'm not talking about your potential Realtor. I'm talking about you, Oh Great Impulsive One. Take your time in choosing a real estate agent. Interview several agents to get a feel for who is prompt in returning your phone calls or emails. Ask pertinent questions about the neighborhood and their experiences with selling in that particular neighborhood. Don't let your excitement overrule your logic. Think things through before you commit to anyone.

It takes months to buy a home. During this time, you'll be working closely (like, 'talking almost daily' close) with your Realtor. You want someone who you vibe with and is easy to get ahold of/talk to. Research your realtor carefully, and err on the side of caution when a realtor uses high-pressure tactics to get you to sign with them quickly.

Chapter 4: The Pre-Approval Process

Before you start anything, you'll want to go through the pre-approval process to get approved for a loan to buy the house. The pre-approval process serves two purposes:

Type of House

It gives you an idea about the type of house that you should be looking at. If you are looking at houses that cost $500,000.00, but only get approved for a $250,000.00 loan, you'll need to look elsewhere for a house that better suits your budget.

Relators

It lets Realtors know that you are serious about buying a home. It's one thing to stroll into a realtor's office to let them know that you're *interested* in purchasing that fancy $1M house that you saw on the way in; it's a whole other animal to have a letter from a lender who is willing to commit to loaning you this $1M.

Submit an offer

Once you start looking for a home and you fall in love with one, you'll be ready to submit an offer.

You'll need to have a pre-approval letter with your offer. Sellers will not want to risk taking their property off the market unless they know that the buyer is fully qualified.

The pre-approval process and the pre-qualification process are sometimes used by lenders to mean the same thing. But, it's always good to know the difference in these terms.

A pre-approval is a firm commitment from a lender that says: "Yes. I will give you x amount of money for your house."

A pre-qualification is a non-committal statement from a lender that says: "I think I can give you x amount of money for your house, but I'm not sure. I need to see more documents and ask more questions. Anyway, maybe I'll give you some money for your house once I get to see that stuff."

Getting a pre-approval letter gives you the confidence that you need to pick a home that's appropriate to your budget.

Here's how the pre-approval process works:

Find a suitable lender

Your lender is the one who will be loaning you money to buy your home. You'll have to deal with this lender for your monthly payments. Depending on your mortgage type, that could be up to 30 years. To that effect, you probably want to find a lender that you ...*like*. Do some research to find a couple of lenders who offer the best interest rates.

Then carefully read reviews on those lenders to determine the best option. Also, research the lender's loan products. Some may offer low down payment options such a no money down, or first time home buyer products.

Apply for a Loan

Once you've found a lender, you apply for a mortgage loan on their website, over the phone, or at their office. You'll have to answer some personal questions, and in some cases, submit some personal financial documentation.

Don't let this discourage you. The lender simply needs to get a better idea of what financial situation you're in so that they know how much money they'll give you. The lender will respond to you promptly, and present you with a pre-approval letter that lists the loan amount that you qualify for. With that loan amount in mind, you and your Realtor will start the process of searching for houses within your budget.

The pre-approval process is not a terribly tedious one. With the right credit score, most lenders will jump at the chance to loan you money and charge interest on the loan. Don't fall for the flattery. Do your research and be meticulous in choosing a lender who best suits your financial needs.

Chapter 5: Loan Options: Choosing the Right Type of Loan for You

If you're looking to buy a home, and you don't have $200,000.00 in cash just lying around in a closet-bound shoebox like the rest of us, getting a lender to loan you the money would be your best bet. There are several types of loans that you can choose from. In general, no particular option is better than the other, but there is an option that's better for *you*. The right loan option allows for a reasonable monthly budget and room to increase your savings. Adversely, the wrong loan option could very well wreck your finances.

Here are four important loan options to consider:

The 30-year fixed option

With this loan type you, the borrower, agree to pay a set amount of money per month for 30 years. Your monthly principle and interest payment will never change throughout the life of the loan, so you don't ever have to worry about your mortgage increasing (except for property tax or HOA fee increases). Homebuyers who either plan to stay in their home for some years or who enjoy the stability that comes with paying a set monthly amount, tend to lean toward this option.

The 15-year fixed option

Similar to the 30-year fixed loan type, the 15-year entire life of the loan (in this case, 15 years). The difference is that your payments will be higher with this loan type than they would with the 30-year fixed option. The reason for this is that the payments are not as spread out as they are with a longer fixed loan option. People who are looking to pay their house off quicker and don't mind the higher monthly payments, tend to go with this loan type. Also, interest rates tend to be lower with the 15 years fixed option in comparison to the 30 years fixed.

The 5/5 ARM (Adjustable Rate Mortgage) option

With a 5/5 ARM, the borrower agrees to pay a fixed amount of money for a total of 5 years. After that five years, your monthly payment will change. The lure to this option is the fact that the 5/5 ARM typically has lower interest rates than the fixed loan options. If you don't plan to stay in your home for longer than five years, this may be a suitable option for you. If you're not sure how long you'll be in your new home, you may want to rethink this option, as you could potentially be responsible for paying an increased mortgage payment in 5 years.

The no money down option/down payment

When you are buying a home, it's customary to put down 20% of the house's cost. However, that can get a tad pricey if you're buying a home of high value. For this reason, there are a couple of ways to avoid paying a down payment on the home altogether. Explore these options with your Realtor & loan officer to find the one that suits you and your needs the best. It's important to note that this option can be combined with any of the fixed rate or 5/5 ARM options.

Choosing the right loan *for you* is an invaluable part of the home-buying process. You will need to assess your needs, and possibly the needs of a spouse or children. Examine the pros and cons to each option and go with the option that will benefit you in the long run.

Chapter 6:
Finding the Right Home

Have you ever been looking for an item while shopping, and then by some miraculous stroke of luck, you find that item in-store? Once you find it, you probably make a subconscious vow to yourself to hold onto that item forever and ever, and never let it get out of your sight again. While this is an admirable attitude to have when you've found the right pair of new shoes, it's probably not a good mindset to have when you're buying a house.

Starter Home

Your first home will likely be what's called a "starter home." Starter homes are exactly what they sound like. They are homes that allow new buyers to transition to a house without having to pay an outlandish amount of money for an outlandish amount of space.

For example, if you're 2-3 years out of college with no children and no spouse, you probably wouldn't need as much space as someone who has a spouse and multiple children. You, the fresh-out-of-college buyer, would purchase a smaller, less expensive home so that you could still reap the benefits of being a homeowner with the unnecessarily high costs.

The last thing that you want to do during this home-buying process is get so attached to a home that you're not willing to consider anything else. Don't get me wrong; you should love the home that you choose. Just don't limit yourself to thinking that there will never, ever be another home suitable for you. That just simply isn't true.

New buyers who don't understand the concept of a starter home typically fall prey to these mindsets:

- "This house is perfectly and divinely constructed to my liking. There will never be another home for me."

- "If I don't get the four-bedroom house with the Jacuzzi and complimentary Butler, then there's no point in buying."

Falling victim to either of these mindsets is a mistake. Understand that your starter home doesn't have to be the grandest, biggest house in the world. Your starter home should be some place that will grow with you over the next five years or so, but try not to get carried away with impressing those around you. Stick to what makes sense for your budget.

Chapter 7: Using Social Media to Find Your New Neighborhood

Having trouble choosing a good neighborhood outside of your own? Social media may be able to help you with that. Social media is a good source for picking people's brains, finding relevant news, and assessing property value. Depending on the platform, you can quickly learn a great deal about some neighborhoods.

These four social media platforms are excellent sources for scoping out neighborhoods:

1. **Facebook:**

Facebook is good for getting a large amount of feedback in a short amount of time. Want to know something specific about a neighborhood? Ask the question in a Facebook status. You can bet that one of your friends will know the answer, and if they don't know, their friend's friend will know. The amount of people who you can reach in just minutes is essentially endless.

2. **Pinterest**

Want to know about a neighborhood and its relevant current events? Using Pinterest might be your best bet. Just enter the name of the neighborhood in the search box and see all of the relevant pins about that area. This is a great way to find out about a neighborhood's current events and market value.

3. **Instagram:**

Are you a person who focuses primarily on the look of a neighborhood? If so, you may find that Instagram can be a useful tool in your neighborhood search. Enter the name of the prospective neighborhood in the search box and look at the images that pop up. Are there any surprises? Things that you see that are deal breakers? People looking to sell their houses sometimes don't post online pictures that actually represent what the house looks like, but Instagram users unknowingly do. The pictures posted to Instagram— particularly ones *not* posted by the seller— will give you the best idea of what type of house and neighborhood you're dealing with.

4. **LinkedIn:**

Are you business-oriented, and thinking about which neighborhood will give you the best bang for your buck? LinkedIn can give you accurate and up-to-date information about the health of a given neighborhood. Just type the neighborhood's name into the search bar to get current event news and profile links to people who live in that neighborhood.

If you're looking for a resource that won't let you down, try searching for a neighborhood by using a popular search engine such as Google or Yahoo. Not only will you get the best of both worlds with tons of images and articles to accompany your keywords, but you'll also have a excellent starting point for knowing which social media platform to utilize.

Chapter 8: From Contract to Closing

To put it lightly, the process of buying a home isn't one that a whole lot of people breeze through with no issues. There are some steps involved—all of which can have unique pitfalls. While there's no way to stop *all* of the issues that you may encounter during the home-buying process, there are ways to minimize some of the more common roadblocks.

So what happens after you've been pre-approved and have found a suitable real estate agent?

Here's what you can expect from the time you sign your contract, all the way to your closing:

Step One: Finding a Home

Once you've gotten your pre-approval letter, it's time to start looking at houses with your realtor. Use the loan amount from your pre-approval letter to set a realistic expectation for what you're looking for in a house.

If you were pre-approved for $160,000.00, it probably bests that you didn't look at that mansion worth $5M. Adversely, if you were pre-approved for $300,000.00, that house that you've been eyeing for $200,000.00 might be realistic for you.

Do you want a condo, a town home, or a single family home? Keep in mind that each of these has their pros and cons. Do you enjoy yardwork and think you can reasonably keep up it? A single family home might be a great choice for you. Or, would you prefer that someone maintained the yard for you? If so, a condo or a townhouse may be more fitting. Think long and hard about what type of home you want to live in for the next five years or so.

Your realtor will help you with this task by suggesting listings to you that fit with what you're looking for. You simply have to view the listings that she sends, and let her know which houses you're interested in viewing. She'll set up an appointment for you and her to view the house.

Step Two: Signing the Purchase Agreement

So you've found a home that you love, and that's suitable for your needs; now it's time to make an offer. Your realtor will help you with the amount that you're going to offer. She will do what's called a CMA (Comparative Market Analysis) to see what other homes in that area are selling for. The amount of money that you offer the seller will largely depend on the CMA and the seller's listing price.

Once negotiations are done, and you and the seller have both agreed on an amount, you will sign a purchase agreement and deliver a deposit. Your realtor can help you decide on a reasonable amount for your deposit. The purchase agreement and deposit are your way of saying: "I'm serious, y'all. I do want this house, and I'm not just making an offer because it's Wednesday."

Both the deposit and the purchase agreement let the seller's side know that your offer is sincere. They also are two things you'll need if you want the seller to take the house off the market. Without the deposit and signed purchase agreement, the seller can keep the house listed and even arrange to have it shown to others.

Step Three: Getting a Home Inspection

Along the way, your lender will ask you for additional documentation that you may not have known you initially needed. That's okay. Submitting additional documentation is a normal part of the home-buying process and one that is almost unavoidable (unless you happen to be clairvoyant and 100% inside of your lender's head). While the lender is conducting their research on *you,* you will want to do research of your own on *the home*.

It's great that you've found a home that's perfect for you and in a great neighborhood; but, there may be underlying issues in your new home that you can't see with the naked eye. Getting a home inspection prevents these *issues* from surprising you later on after you've comfortably settled into your home. It also may give you some leverage to request additional money off the overall price of the home, depending on what your home inspector finds.

You'll have to come out of pocket for this service. The cost of your inspection is independent of your down payment and other closing costs. The price does vary based on location and type of house, but putting aside about $500.00 should cover the bulk, if not all, of your home inspection expenses.

Your Realtor can recommend home inspection companies that other clients have used. If not, use a service such as Angie's List or Yelp to research and read up on home inspection companies that have high ratings. Make sure that the home inspection company services the area that you're moving to.

Step Four: Select Your Loan Type

By now, you should have some vague idea about what exactly your loan type will be. Your options are 30-year fixed, 15-year fixed, and the 5/5 ARM. Now that you've seen your home and know where you'll be moving, it may be easier for you to make this decision.

Have you selected a starter home where you know you'll stay for at least 5-10 years? A fixed mortgage will allow you to keep the same mortgage cost each month. Do you know you'll stay in your starter home for a while, but are strapped for cash? Opting for a longer fixed rate loan option may work for you.

Step Five: Get the Home Appraised

During the underwriting process, your lender will want to have the new property appraised. This is also an expense that is out-of-pocket and independent of the closing costs. To be on the safe side, budget about $500.00 for this process.

An appraisal is simply the lender's official analysis that determines your home's real value independent of what price you've negotiated. The lender will have an independent appraiser come to the house and determine its value. The appraiser takes into account similar homes that have sold and improvements were done to the property. The lender wants to make sure that the house is worth what they're lending to you.

There's nothing that you need to do during the appraisal process short of shelling out the cash for it.

Step Six: The Closing

Your closing is the moment that you've been waiting for. It's when you pay your closing costs, get your keys, and— what *closing costs,* you ask?

Closing costs are fees that are paid at your closing. The amount of these costs vary, but the good news is that your lender will have given you an estimate for closing costs way before closing time comes around. Expect to put no less than 3 % of the purchase price to the side for these costs, although your final amount could be more or less. You're Realtor can also negotiate the closing costs during the purchase agreement period.

During the closing, the title—or, the piece of paper that says you own your house—is turned over to you. You'll sign so many papers that your signature will just start to look like this: ~

But, don't worry. All of the paperwork will be explained to you, and plus, a closing attorney will most likely be at your closing. He or she should be able to answer any questions that you may have.

After all closing costs are paid, and all documents are signed, the keys are handed over to you. And just like that, you're a homeowner!

Chapter 9: Common Pitfalls in the Homebuying Process

As you know by now, the home-buying process is anything but succinct, which means that there is still room for error along the way. The following are some of the common errors that new, millennial homebuyers are susceptible to falling victim to:

- "My cousin has a home just like this one down the street, and his is fine. I don't need a home inspection": Not getting a home inspection is a major mistake. Every house is different. Even if one house doesn't have a problem, another one right next door might. A home inspector examines the nooks and crannies of your house (outside and inside) and may find issues that you can't see such as rodent and termite infestations, a defective roof, issues with mold, and much more. It's always best to be on the safe side and get the home inspection to rule out any huge problems. It's better to spend $500.00 now than to spend $3,000.00 later to correct a problem that could have been detected and fixed before moving in. If you're in a competitive market where most offers you're competing against waive the home inspection, it would be best to get a home inspection before writing up an offer, so you know what you're getting into.

- "I *need* that house. No other house is like it": This statement falls into the mindset that we discussed in previous chapters. Your first home does not have to be *it*. It could very well be your starter home. Focus on living lavishly in your next home when you've had a chance to save up some money and build equity in your first home. For now, it's best to use this time to get on your feet and stay there.

- "My parents said that I should do this to my house, so I'm doing it. What's the big deal?": Keep in mind that *your* name is or will be on the title to your house, not your parents'. That means that *you* are the decision maker. *You* decide whether or not that red chair sitting in the middle of the room is acceptable. *You* decide whether or not your kitchen needs an upgrade, not your parents. It's okay to ask for help or outside opinions. We all need a little advice here and there. But just remember, you aren't *required* to do anything. As a homeowner, you are the game changer. Not your parents.

Avoiding these pitfalls and toxic mindsets can save you a ton of time, money, and hassle down the road.

Chapter 10: Create Ways to Offset Your Mortgage

Having a mortgage doesn't have to mean sacrificing a great deal of money. There are creative ways to offset the cost of a mortgage without having to take on any extra forms of employment.

One smart way to save a ton of money—half of your monthly mortgage payment, to be exact—is to get a roommate.

A roommate will do two things:

Mortgage and Utilities

They'll help cover the mortgage and utilities so that you can save money quickly. In this instance, you'd be able to move out of your starter home and into your dream home a little quicker.

Help in Maintenance

Outside of helping with the financial piece of being a homeowner, a roommate can also help with the general maintenance of the house. Houses tend to be bigger with more space than apartments, so as you can imagine, cleaning a house can be a whole different ball game than cleaning an apartment. But more importantly, a roommate can help maintain the outside of the house. Keeping the outside of the house is just as important as maintaining the inside.

The yard will need to be well manicured, which means weeds will need to be eliminated and the grass will need to be cut. Keeping up with this maintenance is likely to increase the equity in your home, and in turn, the amount of money in your pockets in the long run.

Airbnb

Airbnb is another option for those who are looking to offset mortgage costs. Airbnb is a service that allows people to travel without being dependent on hotels. Travelers simply make arrangements with a host and stay in that host's home or dwelling for a set number of days. Being the host to an Airbnb guest is a great way to earn some extra money on the side to make your mortgage payments.

If you've bought a multi-unit home, there is also the option to rent out a portion of the house. This isn't quite the same thing as having a roommate. A roommate may or may not share rooms with you in the home. Someone who you're renting to, will not share the same space. They'd essentially have their apartment within a house. You, the landlord, would collect a monthly rent payment that could pay all or most of your mortgage costs.

Whether you choose to live with a roommate, use Airbnb, or the renting method, you can take comfort in knowing that any of these options will reduce your monthly mortgage payment. And if you want to come back to any of these options once you've been in the home for a while, it's no sweat. None of the listed options require an immediate upfront commitment when you purchase a home.

When you buy a home, you are taking responsibility and ownership for something that will bring you savings accounts with thousands, a tax shelter, and freedom/flexibility. Making the decision to buy is a big leap, but it's well worth the jump.

Contact Me

Vanessa Patterson
Email: Vanessa.patterson@penfedrealty.com
Telephone no: 202-213-8452